WON-HYO and YUL-KOK
OF TAE KWON DO HYUNG

By JHOON RHEE

Won-Hyo and Yul-Kok are two of the hyungs required
by the International Tae Kwon Do Federation.

OHARA  PUBLICATIONS, INCORPORATED
SANTA CLARITA, CALIFORNIA

I would like to express my sincere appreciation to my photographers,
Mr. Jimmy Rudd
And
Mr. Ku Kyung Chung

WARNING

©Ohara Publications, Incorporated 1971
All rights reserved
Printed in the United States of America
Library of Congress Catalog Card Number: 70-157046
Twenty-second printing 2001
ISBN 0-89750-002-4

PREFACE

Although introduced only recently in the western world, the art of Tae Kwon Do has become increasingly popular in all countries and with all age groups. Originally conceived in Korea as a measure of unarmed self-defense, Tae Kwon Do has blossomed into an art that is now practiced all over the world.

This book has been written with several purposes in mind. First of all, it is intended to develop a greater appreciation and understanding of Tae Kwon Do, which would contribute toward the growth of this ancient martial art. Since it includes explicit instructions and detailed guidance on all aspects of the art, it will serve as a basic text for beginners. To the intermediate students, this text provides a firm foundation for the more complicated patterns and advanced techniques which follow. It also serves as an authoritative reference on all phases of Tae Kwon Do training for the instructors.

WON-HYO and YUL-KOK is the third in a series of five volumes covering nine of the major hyungs of Tae Kwon Do. The first book deals with the Chon-Ji hyung required at the white belt level. The second book deals with Tan-Gun and To-San which are required at the gold belt level. The two hyungs in this book, Won-Hyo and Yul-Kok, are required at the green belt level. The other books in the series will deal with the remaining hyungs required in order to obtain the black belt.

It is my most sincere wish that this book will embody the true essence of Tae Kwon Do—the discipline and humility which arise from one's dedication to the art. Without such spirit, the student's training is incomplete; with it, he becomes master of himself. For both the physical and spiritual fulfillment of Tae Kwon Do, then, this book is humbly dedicated.

Jhoon Rhee

SENATOR MILTON R. YOUNG
President—U.S. Tae Kwon Do Association

AUTHOR JHOON RHEE

CONTENTS

WHAT IS TAE KWON DO?

Tae Kwon Do is a Korean martial art which has been developed through centuries of Eastern civilization. Today Tae Kwon Do has evolved into not only the most effective method of weaponless self-defense but an intricate art, an exciting sport and a trenchant method of maintaining physical fitness.

Many think that breaking boards and bricks is what Tae Kwon Do consists of, but this is an entirely mistaken concept. Demonstrations displaying such feats merely show the power and speed the human body is capable of utilizing through Tae Kwon Do training.

Tremendous skill and control are required in Tae Kwon Do. While blocking, kicking and punching techniques all contribute to making Tae Kwon Do one of the most exciting and competitive sports, its challenge lies in the adept use of techniques without having any actual body contact. Complete control over punching and kicking movements is paramount in stopping just centimeters short of the opponent.

Through the coordination of control, balance and technique in the performance of hyungs (patterns), Tae Kwon Do is regarded as a beautiful and highly skilled martial art. It is also one of the most all-around methods of physical fitness since it utilizes every single muscle of the body and is considered the ultimate in unarmed self-defense. In Korea, the Presidential Protective Forces are all trained in Tae Kwon Do and several other countries are adopting it into the training programs of their protective forces as well.

WHAT ARE TAE KWON DO HYUNGS?

One of the more important aspects of Tae Kwon Do training is learning Tae Kwon Do hyungs, a set series of attacking and defensive movements which follow a logical, predetermined sequence. Although each hyung comprises different movements or techniques, there are certain basic elements common to all:

1) Each hyung begins and ends from the same point.
2) All movements are performed at speeds and rhythms conforming to those established by the hyungs being performed.
3) All movements must be performed with rapid facing and correct posture.

Each hyung in itself is of immense value in the physical and mental development of the student since it serves many purposes. As a means of physical conditioning, it develops the student's balance, muscle coordination and endurance which ultimately leads to increased self-discipline.

Hyungs also give the student the opportunity to practice the ideal blocking and attacking movements against an imaginary opponent. Just as the student in school learns to print, so his handwriting is a departure from the ideal and becomes a mark of his personal style. The same may be said for Tae Kwon Do. A student's sparring or fighting style becomes his adaptation of the principles he has acquired from hyungs. The hyungs, then, are the student's line between Tae Kwon Do training and actual fighting.

Finally, hyungs are a graphic demonstration of the art of Tae Kwon Do that is a mark of the level of development the student has acquired. As a student progresses he undertakes more complex hyungs. They are designed to challenge and make him call upon his resources and all that he has learned in order to perform the new movements and increase his scope of discipline and development.

Tae Kwon Do hyungs have been developed and perfected throughout the centuries by the outstanding teachers of the art. Each hyung consists of the most logical movements of blocking, punching, striking or kicking possible within that sequence of movements. A student should not attempt to take on a new hyung until he has perfected the hyungs he is required to learn at his level of achievement. Before advancing to another hyung it is customary for a student to perform the one he is presently learning at least 300 times.

WITH WHAT HYUNG DOES EACH RANK TRAIN?

HYUNG	RANK (Class)	COLOR BELT	AMOUNT PERFORMED
Chon-Ji	10th & 9th	White	At Least 300 Times
Tan-Gun	8th	Gold	At Least 300 Times
To-San	7th	Gold	At Least 300 Times
Won-Hyo	6th	Green	At Least 300 Times
Yul-Kok	5th	Green	At Least 300 Times
Chung-Gun	4th	Blue	At Least 300 Times
Toi-Gye	3rd	Blue	At Least 300 Times
Hwa-Rang	2nd	Brown	At Least 300 Times
Chung-Mu	1st	Brown	At Least 300 Times

REQUIREMENTS FOR
1ST DEGREE BLACK BELT

1. Right attitude and good character.

2. Mastery of the aforementioned nine patterns.

3. Capability of breaking three, one-inch pine boards with the following techniques:

   a. straight punch

   b. knife hand strike

   c. front or roundhouse kick

   d. side snap kick

4. Good free-sparring ability coupled with well-controlled techniques.

5. Ability and willingness to teach the tenets of Tae Kwon Do to others.

WON-HYO HYUNG

Won-Hyo was the noted monk who introduced Buddhism to the Silla Dynasty in the year 686 A.D.

DIAGRAM

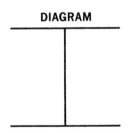

WON-HYO AT A GLANCE

READY   1

6   7   8   9

14   15   16   17

22   23   24   25

| 2 | 3 | 4 | 5 |

| 10 | 11 | 12 | 13 |

| 18 | 19 | 20 | 21 |

| 26 | 27 | 28 | END |

15

SIDE VIEW

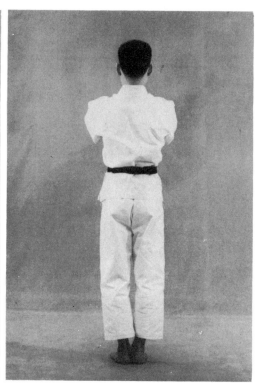

BACK VIEW

OTHER VIEW

STEP DIAGRAM

CHUNBI SOGI
(Ready Stance)

Assume a closed ready stance with left open hand covering right fist at face level.

NOTE: All pivotal turns indicated in degrees, either clockwise or counterclockwise, refer to the directional turn of the face. Star symbols (★) indicate KIHAP (yelling).

FRONT VIEW

TOP VIEW

APPLICATION

17

BEGINNING FRONT VIEW

INTERMEDIATE FRONT VIEW

OTHER VIEW

STEP DIAGRAM

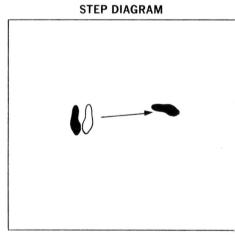

1. SANG PALMOK MARKI

(Twin Forearm Block)

Pivot on the right foot 90 degrees counter-clockwise, assuming a right back stance as you execute a twin forearm block.*

FINAL FRONT VIEW

TOP VIEW

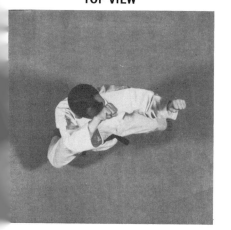

APPLICATION

BEGINNING FRONT VIEW

INTERMEDIATE FRONT VIEW

OTHER VIEW

STEP DIAGRAM

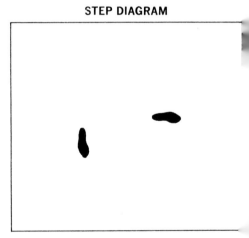

2. SANGDAN SUDO ANURO TAERIGI
(High Knife-Hand Inward Strike)

Execute a high inward strike with the right knife-hand as you bring the left fist to the right shoulder.

FINAL FRONT VIEW

TOP VIEW

APPLICATION

BEGINNING FRONT VIEW

INTERMEDIATE FRONT VIEW

OTHER VIEW

STEP DIAGRAM

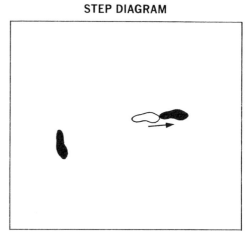

3. CHUNGDAN YOP CHIRUGI
(Middle Side Punch)

Step out to the left with the left foot, assuming a fixed stance as you execute a middle side punch with the left fist.

FINAL FRONT VIEW

TOP VIEW

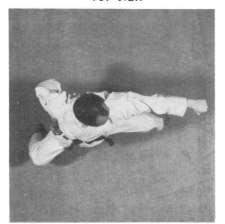

APPLICATION

BEGINNING FRONT VIEW

INTERMEDIATE FRONT VIEW

OTHER VIEW

STEP DIAGRAM

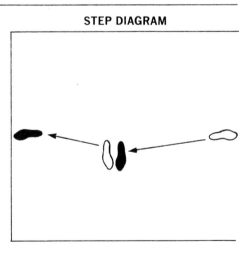

4. SANG PALMOK MARKI
(Twin Forearm Block)

Move the left foot to the right foot, then step out to the right with the right foot, assuming a left back stance as you execute a twin forearm block.

FINAL FRONT VIEW

TOP VIEW

APPLICATION

BEGINNING FRONT VIEW

INTERMEDIATE FRONT VIEW

OTHER VIEW

STEP DIAGRAM

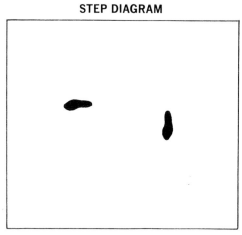

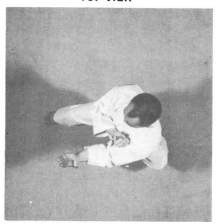

5. SANGDAN SUDO ANURO TAERIGI

(High Knife-Hand Inward Strike)

Execute a high inward strike with the left knife-hand as you bring the right fist to the left shoulder.

FINAL FRONT VIEW

TOP VIEW
APPLICATION

BEGINNING FRONT VIEW

INTERMEDIATE FRONT VIEW

OTHER VIEW

STEP DIAGRAM

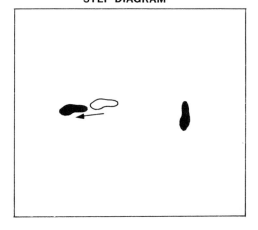

FINAL FRONT VIEW

6. CHUNGDAN YOP CHIRUGI
(Middle Side Punch)

Step out to the right with the right foot, assuming a fixed stance as you execute a middle side punch with the right fist.

TOP VIEW	APPLICATION

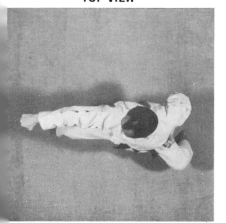

BEGINNING FRONT VIEW

INTERMEDIATE FRONT VIEW

OTHER VIEW

STEP DIAGRAM

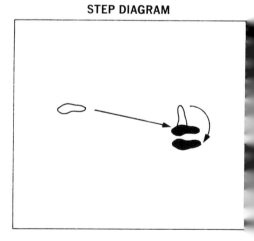

FINAL FRONT VIEW

7. YOP CHAGI CHUNBI SOGI

(Side Kick Ready Stance)

Move the right foot to the left foot, standing up straight as you pivot 90 degrees clockwise on the left heel. Place both fists at the side of the right chest, with your face remaining in the same direction.

TOP VIEW

APPLICATION

BEGINNING FRONT VIEW

INTERMEDIATE FRONT VIEW

OTHER VIEW

STEP DIAGRAM

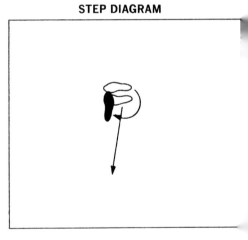

8. CHUNGDAN YOP CHAGI
(Middle Side Thrust Kick)

Execute a middle side thrust kick with the left foot.

FINAL FRONT VIEW

TOP VIEW

APPLICATION

BEGINNING FRONT VIEW

INTERMEDIATE FRONT VIEW

OTHER VIEW

STEP DIAGRAM

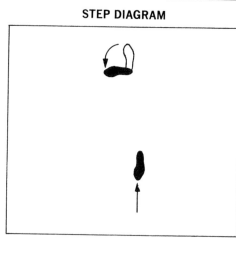

9. CHUNGDAN SUDO MARKI
(Middle Knife-Hand Block)

Take a straight step with the kicking foot, assuming a right back stance as you execute a middle knife-hand guarding block with the left knife-hand.

FINAL FRONT VIEW

TOP VIEW

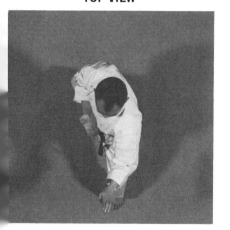

APPLICATION

BEGINNING FRONT VIEW

INTERMEDIATE FRONT VIEW

OTHER VIEW

STEP DIAGRAM

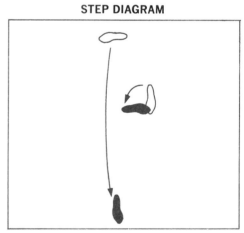

FINAL FRONT VIEW

10. CHUNGDAN SUDO MARKI
(Middle Knife-Hand Block)

Take a straight step with the right foot, assuming a left back stance as you execute a middle knife-hand guarding block with the right knife-hand.

TOP VIEW	APPLICATION

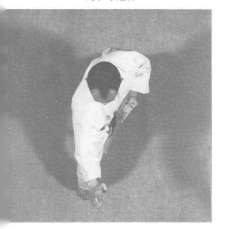

BEGINNING FRONT VIEW   **INTERMEDIATE FRONT VIEW**

OTHER VIEW   **STEP DIAGRAM**

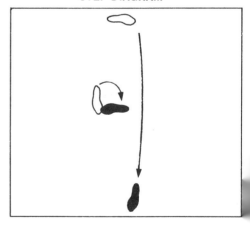

11. CHUNGDAN SUDO MARKI
(Middle Knife-Hand Block)

Take a straight step with the left foot, assuming a right back stance as you execute a middle knife-hand guarding block with the left knife-hand.

FINAL FRONT VIEW

TOP VIEW   **APPLICATION**

BEGINNING FRONT VIEW

INTERMEDIATE FRONT VIEW

OTHER VIEW

STEP DIAGRAM

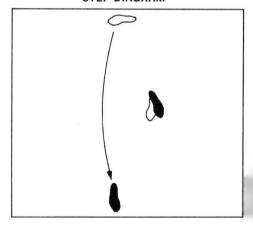

★

12. CHUNGDAN KWANSU

(Middle Spear Finger)

Take a straight step with the right foot, assuming a right front stance as you execute a vertical spear finger thrust with the right hand.✶

FINAL FRONT VIEW

TOP VIEW

APPLICATION

41

BEGINNING FRONT VIEW

INTERMEDIATE FRONT VIEW

OTHER VIEW

STEP DIAGRAM

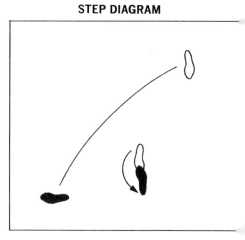

13. SANG PALMOK MARKI

(Twin Forearm Block)

Pivot on the right foot 270 degrees counter-clockwise, assuming a right back stance as you execute a twin forearm block.

FINAL FRONT VIEW

TOP VIEW

APPLICATION

BEGINNING FRONT VIEW   **INTERMEDIATE FRONT VIEW**

OTHER VIEW   **STEP DIAGRAM**

14. SANGDAN SUDO ANURO TAERIGI

(High Knife-Hand Inward Strike)

Execute a high inward strike with the right knife-hand as you bring the left fist to the right shoulder.

FINAL FRONT VIEW

TOP VIEW

APPLICATION

45

BEGINNING FRONT VIEW

INTERMEDIATE FRONT VIEW

OTHER VIEW

STEP DIAGRAM

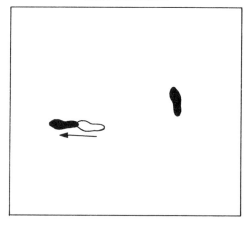

46

15. CHUNGDAN YOP CHIRUGI
(Middle Side Punch)

Step out to the left with the left foot, assuming a fixed stance as you execute a middle side punch with the left fist.

FINAL FRONT VIEW

TOP VIEW

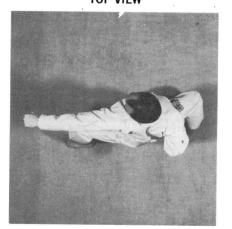

APPLICATION

BEGINNING FRONT VIEW

INTERMEDIATE FRONT VIEW

OTHER VIEW

STEP DIAGRAM

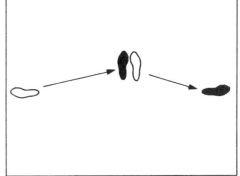

16. SANG PALMOK MARKI
(Twin Forearm Block)

Move the left foot to the right foot, then step out to the right with the right foot, assuming a left back stance as you execute a twin forearm block.

FINAL FRONT VIEW

TOP VIEW

APPLICATION

BEGINNING FRONT VIEW

INTERMEDIATE FRONT VIEW

OTHER VIEW

STEP DIAGRAM

FINAL FRONT VIEW

17. SANGDAN SUDO ANURO TAERIGI

(High Knife-Hand Inward Strike)

Execute a high inward strike with the left knife-hand as you bring the right fist to the left shoulder.

TOP VIEW

APPLICATION

BEGINNING FRONT VIEW　　　　**INTERMEDIATE FRONT VIEW**

OTHER VIEW　　　　**STEP DIAGRAM**

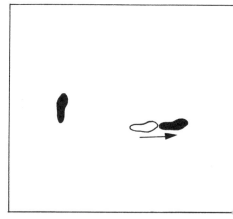

52

FINAL FRONT VIEW

18. CHUNGDAN YOP CHIRUGI
(Middle Side Punch)

Step out to the right with the right foot, assuming a fixed stance as you execute a middle side punch with the right fist.

TOP VIEW	**APPLICATION**

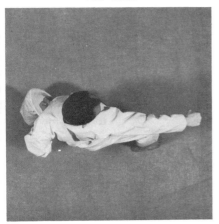

BEGINNING FRONT VIEW

INTERMEDIATE FRONT VIEW

OTHER VIEW

STEP DIAGRAM

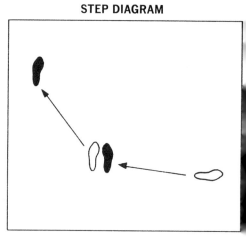

19. ANPALMOK TOLYO MARKI

(Inner Wrist Circular Block)

Move the right foot to the left foot, then take a straight step with the left foot, assuming a left front stance as you execute a circular block with the right inner wrist.

FINAL FRONT VIEW

TOP VIEW

APPLICATION

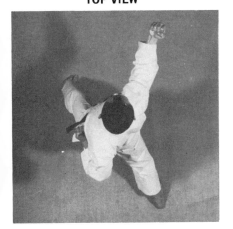

OTHER VIEW

STEP DIAGRAM

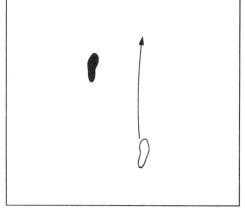

20. CHUNGDAN AP CHAGI
(Middle Front Snap Kick)

Execute a middle front snap kick with the right foot without changing hand positions.

FINAL FRONT VIEW

TOP VIEW

APPLICATION

BEGINNING FRONT VIEW

INTERMEDIATE FRONT VIEW

OTHER VIEW

STEP DIAGRAM

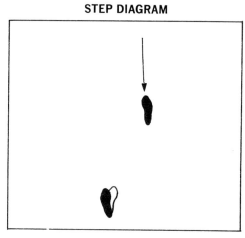

FINAL FRONT VIEW

21. CHUNGDAN PANDAE CHIRUGI

(Middle Reverse Punch)

Take a straight step with the kicking foot, assuming a right front stance as you execute a middle reverse punch with the left fist.

TOP VIEW   **APPLICATION**

BEGINNING FRONT VIEW

OTHER VIEW

INTERMEDIATE FRONT VIEW

STEP DIAGRAM

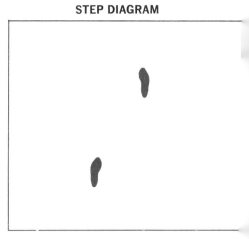

FINAL FRONT VIEW

22. ANPALMOK TOLYO MARKI

(Inner Wrist Circular Block)

Execute a circular block with the left inner wrist.

TOP VIEW

APPLICATION

STEP DIAGRAM

 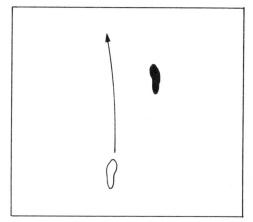

23. CHUNGDAN AP CHAGI
(Middle Front Snap Kick)

Execute a middle front snap kick with the left foot without changing hand positions.

FINAL FRONT VIEW

TOP VIEW

APPLICATION

BEGINNING FRONT VIEW

INTERMEDIATE FRONT VIEW

OTHER VIEW

STEP DIAGRAM

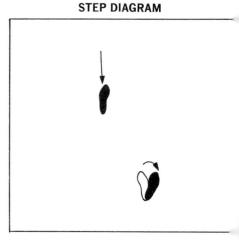

24. CHUNGDAN PANDAE CHIRUGI
(Middle Reverse Punch)

Take a straight step with the kicking foot, assuming a left front stance as you execute a middle reverse punch with the right fist.

FINAL FRONT VIEW

TOP VIEW

APPLICATION

BEGINNING FRONT VIEW

INTERMEDIATE FRONT VIEW

OTHER VIEW

STEP DIAGRAM

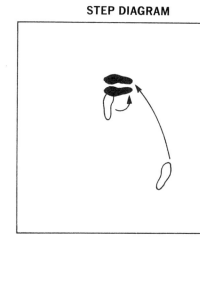

FINAL FRONT VIEW

25. YOP CHAGI CHUNBI SOGI
(Side Kick Ready Stance)

Move the right foot to the left foot, then stand straight up as you pivot on the left heel 90 degrees counterclockwise with both fists placed at the side of the left chest.

| TOP VIEW | APPLICATION |

BEGINNING FRONT VIEW

INTERMEDIATE FRONT VIEW

OTHER VIEW

STEP DIAGRAM

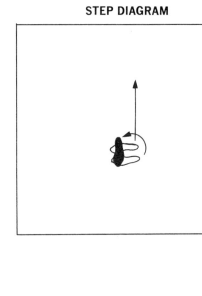

26. CHUNGDAN YOP CHAGI
(Middle Side Thrust Kick)

Execute a middle side thrust kick with the right foot.

FINAL FRONT VIEW

TOP VIEW

APPLICATION

69

BEGINNING FRONT VIEW

INTERMEDIATE FRONT VIEW

OTHER VIEW

STEP DIAGRAM

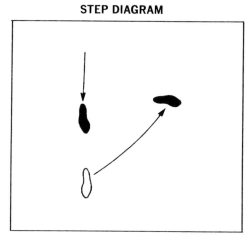

FINAL FRONT VIEW

27. CHUNGDAN PALMOK MARKI

(Middle Forearm Block)

Lower the kicking foot in front of the body, then pivot on the right foot 270 degrees counterclockwise, assuming a right back stance as you execute a middle forearm guarding block with the left arm.

TOP VIEW

APPLICATION

BEGINNING FRONT VIEW

INTERMEDIATE FRONT VIEW

OTHER VIEW

STEP DIAGRAM

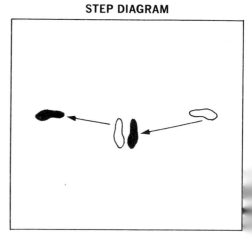

28. CHUNGDAN PALMOK MARKI
(Middle Forearm Block)

Move the left foot to the right foot, then step out to the right with the right foot, assuming a left back stance as you execute a middle forearm guarding block with the right arm, the face turned 180 degrees clockwise.*

FINAL FRONT VIEW

TOP VIEW

APPLICATION

SIDE VIEW

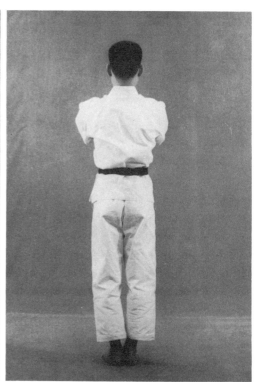

BACK VIEW

OTHER VIEW

STEP DIAGRAM

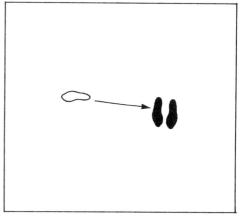

GOMAN
(End)

Bring the right foot toward the left, assuming a closed ready stance with left open hand covering right fist at face level.

FRONT VIEW

TOP VIEW

APPLICATION

YUL-KOK HYUNG

Yul-Kok is the pseudonym of a great philosopher and scholar, Yi I (1536-1584 A.D.), who was nicknamed the "Confucius of Korea". The 38 movements of this pattern represent the 38 degrees latitude of Yul-Kok's birthplace, and the Diagram represents "scholar".

DIAGRAM

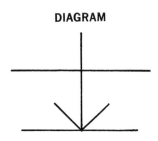

YUL-KOK AT A GLANCE

READY   1   2   3   4

10   11   12   13   14

20   21   22   23   24

30   31   32   33   34

SIDE VIEW

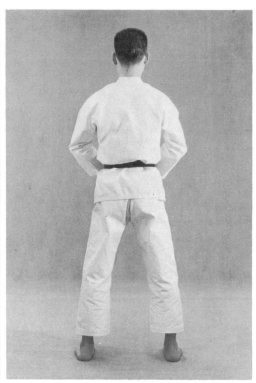

BACK VIEW

OTHER VIEW

STEP DIAGRAM

FRONT VIEW

CHUNBI SOGI
(Ready Stance)

Assume a parallel ready stance.

NOTE: All pivotal turns indicated in degrees, either clockwise or counterclockwise, refer to the directional turn of the face. Star symbols (★) indicate KIHAP (yelling).

TOP VIEW

APPLICATION

BEGINNING FRONT VIEW   **INTERMEDIATE FRONT VIEW**

OTHER VIEW   **STEP DIAGRAM**

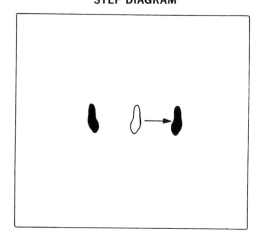

1. CHUNGDAN CHUMOK BUTCHIGI
(Middle Fist Extension)

Step out to the left with the left foot, assuming a riding stance as you execute a slow middle punch with the left fist. The arms should move in a smooth action.

FINAL FRONT VIEW

TOP VIEW	APPLICATION

OTHER VIEW

STEP DIAGRAM

 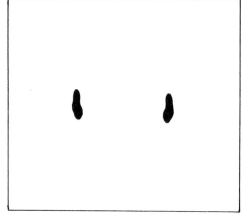

2. CHUNGDAN KIMA SOGI CHIRUGI
(Middle Riding-Stance Punch)

Execute a middle punch with the right fist.

FINAL FRONT VIEW

TOP VIEW	**APPLICATION**

OTHER VIEW

STEP DIAGRAM

FINAL FRONT VIEW

3. CHUNGDAN
KIMA SOGI CHIRUGI
(Middle Riding-Stance Punch)

Execute a middle punch with the left fist.

TOP VIEW	APPLICATION

BEGINNING FRONT VIEW

INTERMEDIATE FRONT VIEW

OTHER VIEW

STEP DIAGRAM

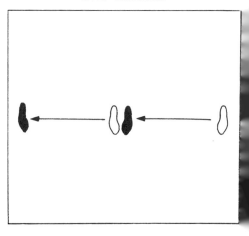

4. CHUNGDAN CHUMOK BUTCHIGI
(Middle Fist Extension)

Bring the left foot alongside the right foot, then step out to the right with the right foot, assuming a riding stance as you execute a slow middle punch with the right fist. The arms should move in a smooth action.

FINAL FRONT VIEW

TOP VIEW	APPLICATION

OTHER VIEW

STEP DIAGRAM

FINAL FRONT VIEW

5. CHUNGDAN KIMA SOGI CHIRUGI
(Middle Riding-Stance Punch)

Execute a middle punch with the left fist.

TOP VIEW

APPLICATION

OTHER VIEW

STEP DIAGRAM

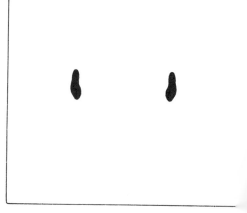

6. CHUNGDAN KIMA SOGI CHIRUGI

(Middle Riding-Stance Punch)

Execute a middle punch with the right fist.

FINAL FRONT VIEW

TOP VIEW	APPLICATION

BEGINNING FRONT VIEW **INTERMEDIATE FRONT VIEW**

OTHER VIEW **STEP DIAGRAM**

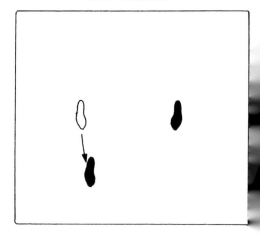

7. SANGDAN ANPALMOK MARKI

(High Inner-Wrist Block)

Pivot on the left foot 45 degrees clockwise, assuming a right front stance as you execute a high inner-wrist block with the right arm.

FINAL FRONT VIEW

TOP VIEW

APPLICATION

OTHER VIEW

STEP DIAGRAM

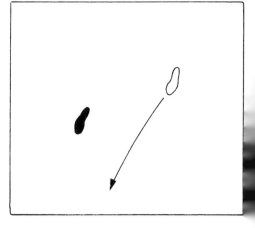

8. CHUNGDAN AP CHAGI
(Middle Front Snap Kick)

Execute a middle front snap kick with the left foot without changing hand positions.

FINAL FRONT VIEW

TOP VIEW   **APPLICATION**

BEGINNING FRONT VIEW   **INTERMEDIATE FRONT VIEW**

OTHER VIEW   **STEP DIAGRAM**

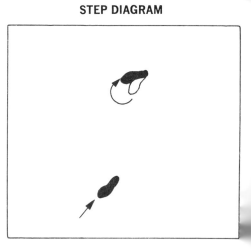

FINAL FRONT VIEW

9. CHUNGDAN CHIRUGI
(Middle Punch)

Take a straight step with the kicking foot, assuming a left front stance as you execute a middle punch with the left fist.

TOP VIEW

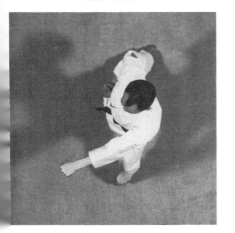

APPLICATION

OTHER VIEW

STEP DIAGRAM

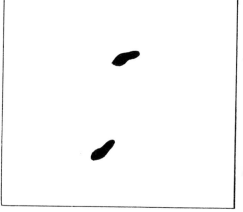

10. CHUNGDAN PANDAE CHIRUGI
(Middle Reverse Punch)

Execute a middle reverse punch with the right fist.

FINAL FRONT VIEW

| TOP VIEW | APPLICATION |

BEGINNING FRONT VIEW

OTHER VIEW

INTERMEDIATE FRONT VIEW

STEP DIAGRAM

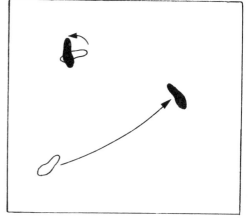

11. SANGDAN ANPALMOK MARKI

(High Inner-Wrist Block)

Pivot on the right foot 90 degrees counter-clockwise, assuming a left front stance as you execute a high inner-wrist block with the left arm.

FINAL FRONT VIEW

TOP VIEW	**APPLICATION**

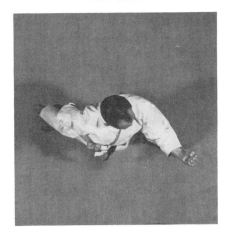

OTHER VIEW

STEP DIAGRAM

 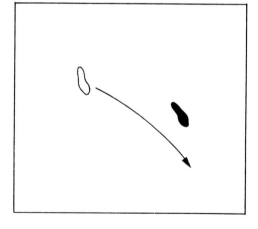

12. CHUNGDAN AP CHAGI

(Middle Front Snap Kick)

Execute a middle front snap kick with the right foot without changing hand positions.

FINAL FRONT VIEW

TOP VIEW

APPLICATION

BEGINNING FRONT VIEW

OTHER VIEW

INTERMEDIATE FRONT VIEW

STEP DIAGRAM

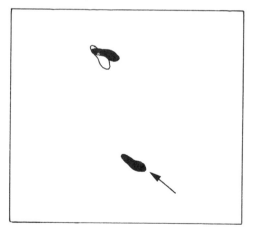

13. CHUNGDAN CHIRUGI
(Middle Punch)

Take a straight step with the kicking foot, assuming a right front stance as you execute a middle punch with the right fist.

FINAL FRONT VIEW

TOP VIEW	APPLICATION

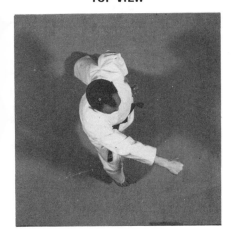

OTHER VIEW

STEP DIAGRAM

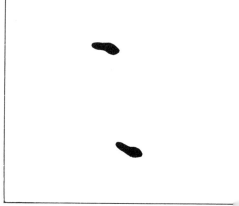

FINAL FRONT VIEW

14. CHUNGDAN PANDAE CHIRUGI
(Middle Reverse Punch)

Execute a middle reverse punch with the left fist.

TOP VIEW

APPLICATION

BEGINNING FRONT VIEW

INTERMEDIATE FRONT VIEW

OTHER VIEW

STEP DIAGRAM

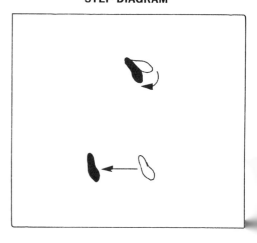

15. SANGDAN SUDO GAULCHO MARKI

(High Knife-Hand Hooking Block)

Pivot on the left foot 45 degrees clockwise, assuming a right front stance as you execute a high hooking block with the right knife-hand. The arms should be moved in a smooth action.

FINAL FRONT VIEW

TOP VIEW

APPLICATION

BEGINNING FRONT VIEW **INTERMEDIATE FRONT VIEW**

OTHER VIEW **STEP DIAGRAM**

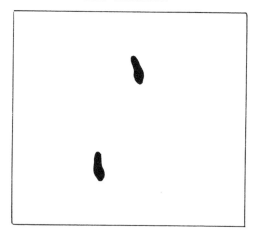

16. SANGDAN SUDO GAULCHO MARKI

(High Knife-Hand Hooking Block)

Execute a high hooking block with the left knife-hand, moving the arms in a smooth action.

FINAL FRONT VIEW

TOP VIEW	APPLICATION

OTHER VIEW	STEP DIAGRAM

 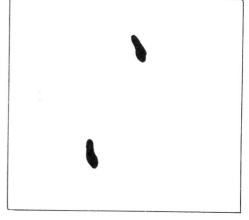

17. CHUNGDAN CHIRUGI

(Middle Punch)

Execute a middle punch with the right fist.

FINAL FRONT VIEW

TOP VIEW	APPLICATION

BEGINNING FRONT VIEW

OTHER VIEW

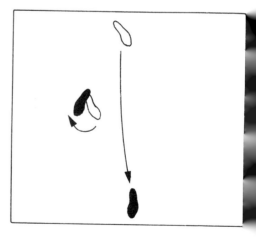

INTERMEDIATE FRONT VIEW

STEP DIAGRAM

18. SANGDAN SUDO GAULCHO MARKI

(High Knife-Hand Hooking Block)

Take a straight step with the left foot, assuming a left front stance as you execute a high hooking block with the left knife-hand. The arms should move in a smooth action.

FINAL FRONT VIEW

TOP VIEW

APPLICATION

BEGINNING FRONT VIEW　　　　**INTERMEDIATE FRONT VIEW**

OTHER VIEW　　　　**STEP DIAGRAM**

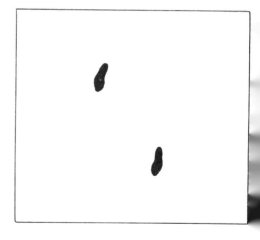

19. SANGDAN SUDO GAULCHO MARKI

(High Knife-Hand Hooking Block)

Execute a high hooking block with the right knife-hand, moving the arms in a smooth action.

FINAL FRONT VIEW

TOP VIEW

APPLICATION

OTHER VIEW

STEP DIAGRAM

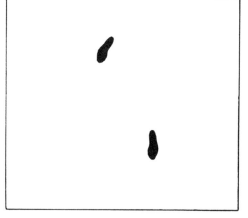

20. CHUNGDAN CHIRUGI
(Middle Punch)

Execute a middle punch with the left fist.

FINAL FRONT VIEW

TOP VIEW	**APPLICATION**

BEGINNING FRONT VIEW

INTERMEDIATE FRONT VIEW

OTHER VIEW

STEP DIAGRAM

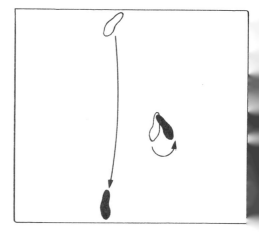

21. CHUNGDAN CHIRUGI
(Middle Punch)

Take a straight step with the right foot, assuming a right front stance as you execute a middle punch with the right fist.✦

FINAL FRONT VIEW

TOP VIEW	APPLICATION

BEGINNING FRONT VIEW

OTHER VIEW

INTERMEDIATE FRONT VIEW

STEP DIAGRAM

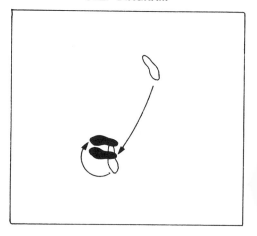

22. YOP CHAGI CHUNBI SOGI
(Side Kick Ready Stance)

Move the left foot to the right foot, then stand up straight as you pivot 90 degrees clockwise on the right heel. Place both fists at the side of the right chest, with your face remaining in the same direction.

FINAL FRONT VIEW

TOP VIEW   **APPLICATION**

BEGINNING FRONT VIEW

INTERMEDIATE FRONT VIEW

OTHER VIEW

STEP DIAGRAM

23. CHUNGDAN YOP CHAGI
(Middle Side Thrust Kick)

Execute a middle side thrust kick with the left foot.

FINAL FRONT VIEW

TOP VIEW

APPLICATION

BEGINNING FRONT VIEW

OTHER VIEW

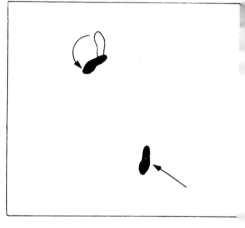

INTERMEDIATE FRONT VIEW

STEP DIAGRAM

24. CHUNGDAN PALKUMCHI TAERIGI
(Middle Elbow Strike)

Take a straight step with the kicking foot, assuming a left front stance as you strike the left palm with the right elbow.

FINAL FRONT VIEW

TOP VIEW	APPLICATION

BEGINNING FRONT VIEW

INTERMEDIATE FRONT VIEW

OTHER VIEW

STEP DIAGRAM

25. YOP CHAGI CHUNBI SOGI

(Side Kick Ready Stance)

Move the right foot to the left foot, then stand up straight as you pivot 90 degrees clockwise on the left heel. Place both fists at the side of the left chest and turn your face 180 degrees clockwise.

FINAL FRONT VIEW

TOP VIEW   **APPLICATION**

BEGINNING FRONT VIEW

INTERMEDIATE FRONT VIEW

OTHER VIEW

STEP DIAGRAM

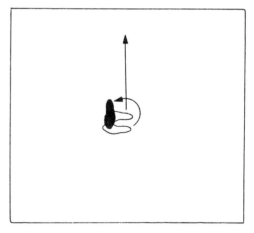

132

26. CHUNGDAN YOP CHAGI

(Middle Side Thrust Kick)

Execute a middle side thrust kick with the right foot.

FINAL FRONT VIEW

TOP VIEW   **APPLICATION**

BEGINNING FRONT VIEW | **INTERMEDIATE FRONT VIEW**

OTHER VIEW | **STEP DIAGRAM**

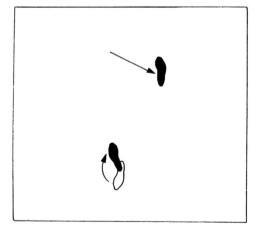

FINAL FRONT VIEW

27. CHUNGDAN PALKUMCHI TAERIGI
(Middle Elbow Strike)

Take a straight step with the kicking foot, assuming a right front stance as you strike the right palm with the left elbow.

TOP VIEW	APPLICATION

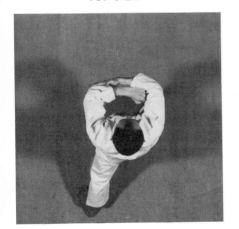

BEGINNING FRONT VIEW

INTERMEDIATE FRONT VIEW

OTHER VIEW

STEP DIAGRAM

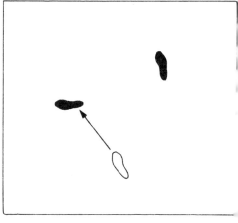

28. SANG SUDO MARKI

(Twin Knife-Hand Block)

Step out to the left with the left foot, assuming a right back stance as you execute a twin knife-hand block.

FINAL FRONT VIEW

TOP VIEW

APPLICATION

BEGINNING FRONT VIEW

INTERMEDIATE FRONT VIEW

OTHER VIEW

STEP DIAGRAM

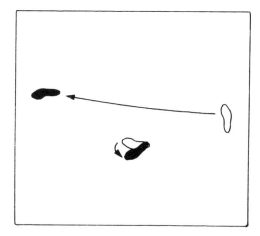

29. CHUNGDAN CHONG KWANSU
(Middle Vertical Spear Finger)

Take a straight step with the right foot, assuming a right front stance as you execute a vertical spear finger thrust with the right hand.

FINAL FRONT VIEW

TOP VIEW

APPLICATION

BEGINNING FRONT VIEW

INTERMEDIATE FRONT VIEW

OTHER VIEW

STEP DIAGRAM

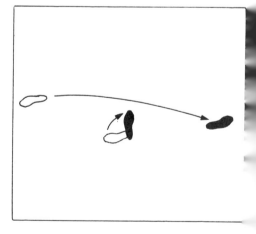

140

30. SANG SUDO MARKI
(Twin Knife-Hand Block)

Pivot on the left foot 180 degrees clockwise, assuming a left back stance as you execute a twin knife-hand block.

FINAL FRONT VIEW

TOP VIEW	**APPLICATION**

BEGINNING FRONT VIEW

INTERMEDIATE FRONT VIEW

OTHER VIEW

STEP DIAGRAM

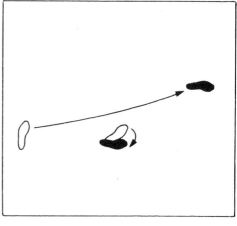

31. CHUNGDAN CHONG KWANSU
(Middle Vertical Spear Finger)

Take a straight step with the left foot, assuming a left front stance as you execute a vertical spear finger thrust with the left hand.

FINAL FRONT VIEW

TOP VIEW	APPLICATION

BEGINNING FRONT VIEW

INTERMEDIATE FRONT VIEW

OTHER VIEW

STEP DIAGRAM

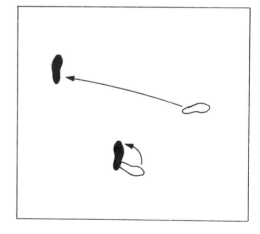

32. SANGDAN PALMOK MARKI

(High Forearm Block)

Pivot on the right foot 90 degrees counter-clockwise, assuming a left front stance as you execute a high block with the left forearm.

FINAL FRONT VIEW

TOP VIEW

APPLICATION

OTHER VIEW

STEP DIAGRAM

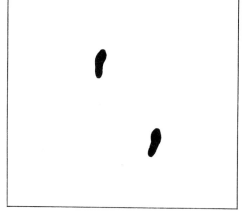

33. CHUNGDAN PANDAE CHIRUGI
(Middle Reverse Punch)

Execute a middle reverse punch with the right fist.

FINAL FRONT VIEW

TOP VIEW	APPLICATION

BEGINNING FRONT VIEW

INTERMEDIATE FRONT VIEW

OTHER VIEW

STEP DIAGRAM

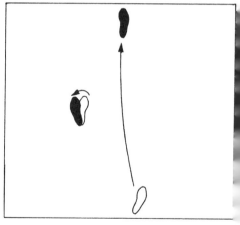

34. SANGDAN PALMOK MARKI
(High Forearm Block)

Take a straight step with the right foot, assuming a right front stance as you execute a high block with the right forearm.

FINAL FRONT VIEW

TOP VIEW	APPLICATION

149

OTHER VIEW

STEP DIAGRAM

 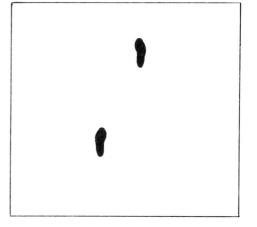

35. CHUNGDAN PANDAE CHIRUGI
(Middle Reverse Punch)

Execute a middle reverse punch with the left fist.

FINAL FRONT VIEW

TOP VIEW	APPLICATION

BEGINNING FRONT VIEW

INTERMEDIATE FRONT VIEW

OTHER VIEW

STEP DIAGRAM

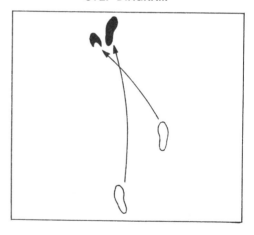

36. SANGDAN YIKWON TAERIGI
(High Back Fist Strike)

Jump forward, landing in a left X stance as you execute a high back fist strike with the left hand. ✦

FINAL FRONT VIEW

TOP VIEW	APPLICATION

BEGINNING FRONT VIEW

INTERMEDIATE FRONT VIEW

OTHER VIEW

STEP DIAGRAM

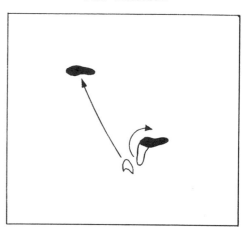

37. SANGDAN DO PALMOK MARKI

(High Double Forearm Block)

Pivot on the left foot 270 degrees clockwise, assuming a right front stance as you execute a high double forearm block.

FINAL FRONT VIEW

TOP VIEW	APPLICATION

BEGINNING FRONT VIEW

INTERMEDIATE FRONT VIEW

OTHER VIEW

STEP DIAGRAM

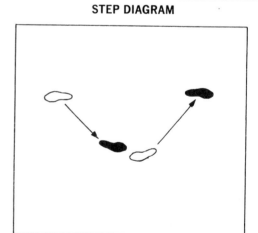

38. SANGDAN DO PALMOK MARKI

(High Double Forearm Block)

Bring the right foot alongside the left foot, then step out with the left foot, assuming a left front stance as you execute a high double forearm block with an 180-degree face turn. ✦

FINAL FRONT VIEW

| TOP VIEW | APPLICATION |

SIDE VIEW

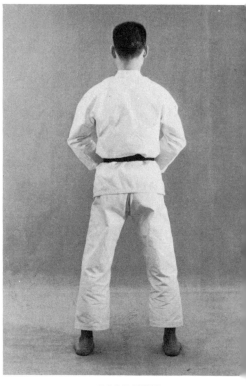

BACK VIEW

OTHER VIEW

STEP DIAGRAM

GOMAN
(End)

Bring the left foot toward the right, assuming a parallel ready stance.

FRONT VIEW

TOP VIEW

APPLICATION